The
Lighter Side of Classroom Management

The
Lighter Side of
Classroom
Management

Aaron Bacall

CORWIN PRESS
A SAGE Publications Company
Thousand Oaks, CA 91320

For information:

Corwin Press
A Sage Publications Company
2455 Teller Road
Thousand Oaks, California 91320
www.corwinpress.com

Sage Publications Ltd.
1 Oliver's Yard
55 City Road
London EC1Y 1SP
United Kingdom

Sage Publications India Pvt. Ltd.
B-42, Panchsheel Enclave
Post Box 4109
New Delhi 110 017 India

Printed in the United States of America.

Library of Congress Cataloging-in-Publication Data

Bacall, Aaron.
The lighter side of classroom management / Aaron Bacall.
    p. cm.
ISBN-13: 978-1-4129-2701-7 (cloth : alk. paper)
ISBN-13: 978-1-4129-2702-4 (pbk. : alk. paper)
    1. American wit and humor, Pictorial. 2. Classroom management—Caricatures and cartoons. I. Title.

NC1429.B127A4 2007
741.5′6973—dc22

                                                                    2006049175
This book is printed on acid-free paper.

06   07   08   09   10   10   9   8   7   6   5   4   3   2   1

Acquisitions Editor: Elizabeth Brenkus
Editorial Assistant: Desirée Enayati
Production Editor: Jenn Reese
Typesetter: C&M Digitals (P) Ltd.
Cover Designer: Michael Dubowe

Introduction

B y definition, classroom learning occurs in a learning environment. That environment can enhance or diminish the educational process. There are a myriad of managerial techniques for improving the classroom setting, but most important is the teacher's attitude. An audience, regardless of age, senses that attitude and responds accordingly. Did the teacher plan well, or is she winging it? Is the teacher enthusiastic, respectful, innovative, nurturing, spontaneous, and empathetic, or is the teacher robotic?

A teacher must remember that he or she is not a teacher of reading, or a teacher of science, or a teacher of history, but a teacher of children. Each child comes to class with a set of perceptions, experiences, and expectations. Each instance of misbehavior has a reason and the teacher has to be able to rely upon a collection of options that can be used to correct that behavior. A teacher has to know when to bend the rules for incidental misbehavior and know when to refer such misbehavior to a school counselor, psychologist, security guard, nurse, or administrator.

A teacher can write a great lesson plan, arrange the seating, adjust the window shades, have an appropriate assignment on the board, start the class on time, and teach to the bell, but that will not necessarily guarantee success.

An effective teacher must do more than enforce behavioral norms. The teacher must walk among the students and overwhelm them with encouragement and attention. The effective teacher must be nurturing and accessible. The effective teacher must extend an invitation to success.

It may sound obvious, but many students come to class with no clear guidelines for appropriate classroom behavior. I have found that to be true even among college students. What we may consider less than respectful behavior may seem entirely appropriate to many students. They need clearly articulated parameters of appropriate behavior in a classroom setting.

Teaching is a noble profession. Maintain positive expectations, and always extend an invitation to success. Always remember that students can read a dour face and behave accordingly. Be upbeat and enthusiastic. Smile! If you need encouragement in that department, read the cartoons in this book. There is a lighter side to classroom management.

—Aaron Bacall

About the Author

Aaron
Bacall

Aaron Bacall's works have appeared in many publications: *The School Administrator, Technology & Learning, The New Yorker, The Wall Street Journal, Barron's,* and *Reader's Digest.* In addition, his work appears in many cartoon books published by Harper and Row, Dow Jones, Bloomberg Press, Contemporary Books (Tribune News Media), and Harper Perennial (HarperCollins publishers), and in advertising. He has worked as a teacher, a principal curriculum writer for the New York City Board of Education, an antibiotic research chemist, and now as a full-time cartoonist and the coordinator of medical programs in continuing education at the College of Staten Island in New York. Three of his cartoons are now part of the Baker Library's Historical Collections Department of The Harvard Business School.

To my favorite e-mail pals
Ben and Em

To my love and inspiration
Linda

To my favorite couple
DAB and Barbara
A perfect match

The Lighter
Side of Classroom
Management

"My biology teacher said I was becoming a pain in the gluteus maximus, whatever that is."

"I can't sign that behavior contract unless my attorney reviews it."

"For throwing spitballs in class, I am sending you
to the principal's office. It's nothing personal.
It's just a classroom management thing."

"My objective is to have each student become more insightful, compassionate, introspective, and empathetic. In your case I will settle for quiet."

"Are you trying to maintain class control with eye contact, or are your contact lenses bothering you?"

"Maybe little Jack Horner became argumentative
because he was backed into a corner,
leaving him no options."

"I have a plan 'B', but that's also dependent on a working projector bulb."

**"You can't just get up and leave
without permission."**

"I want you to sit up front right by my desk. It's not because I want to keep an eye on you. It's a feng shui thing."

**"What do I do? I'm a high stress teacher.
I mean a high school teacher."**

"There are two concerns I have. Your son disturbs the class every day except Friday, and your son always cuts class on Friday."

"I tried everything to get my class to pay attention. I tried bribes, sarcasm, guilt, shame, and threats. Nothing works! Are you paying attention to what I'm saying?"

"I'm alphabetized out! I have arranged
my classroom seating in a 'U', a 'C', an 'O',
and an 'H' configuration and I still have
problems with classroom management."

**"Your classroom management techniques work
in practice but not in theory. That worries me."**

**"I wasn't calling out in class. I was
giving a shout out to my classmates."**

"Your son pays attention in class, but only to his iPod and cell phone."

"You think I'm disrespectful. Right! Now you're cutting into my recess time, so let's just cut to the chase."

"I finally discovered how to stop playground fighting. I forbid students from discussing politics during recess."

"I would appreciate it if you don't call out in class."

"I think I need a good book on classroom management. My class went from The Learning Channel to The Jerry Springer Show in one week."

**"I replaced the clerk's bell with this gong.
Now I have no problem getting the attention
of all my students."**

"It's a bag of masks. I wear them to convey that a particular misbehavior was not overlooked."

"After you grade my report, may I have my
intellectual property back?"

"Did I throw <u>which</u> spitball?"

"I have your school record and I couldn't help noticing that you chewed gum and were tardy and often disruptive in first grade."

**"I find the best palliative technique
to relieve job-related tension and anxiety
is to call in sick."**

"I keep the class on task through inexpensive
incentives. Last week I gave out some
8-track tapes and a few wide neckties that
I purchased on eBay."

"Before you continue your emotional tirade, let me know if you're picking up on my nonevaluative and empathetic listening."

A.BACALL

"I give the same advice to all new teachers. Pretend you know what you are doing."

"I need five weekly lesson plan books. Not only do I tend to overplan, but I feel more comfortable with contingency plans."

"If the key to effective classroom management is consistency, I guess I'm an effective classroom manager. I am consistently exhausted at the end of the day."

"Luck is when good classroom management skills meets a day when the disruptive students are absent."

"Before I begin today's lesson, please turn off your cell phones, beepers, and iPods."

"As part of my classroom management, I try to rotate computer use with other teachers by using a rolling cart. What I didn't plan on was rolling blackouts. All our computers are down."

"Will the student making those disruptive sounds stop? Fair warning! I am gathering evidence and I'm wearing a wire."

"I started to add anecdotal notes about each student's behavior to my grade book. Now the book is too heavy to lift."

"I tried unsuccessfully to deal with a student's behavior. Then I got creative. One day I asked him to help me test the school's transfer policy, and . . . voilà!"

"Now that you learned how to handle difficult
students, you will have to learn how to
handle difficult colleagues."

"Let me have the water gun, Jerome! I'm trying to maintain a sunny disposition and you are raining on my parade."

"I channeled John Dewey. He says if you want to be a good teacher, don't teach reading and writing. Teach students."

"I keep a cold pack in my desk drawer to help me cool my emotions before I approach an argumentative student."

**"I always hold my cat when I teach.
It calms me, and the class, down."**

"My fortune says, 'You will be successful in getting students to control their behavior, if you first control your own behavior'."

"I am going to close my eyes and cover my ears. I expect the student who took my chair, my desk, and my chalkboard to bring them back."

**"I will not tolerate any misbehavior
in this school!"**

"The last one to quiet down is a rotten egg."

"Obedience school was okay, but the teacher responded to my unwanted behavior with penalties. I never learned any long-term behavior modification, so I'm still barking and ignoring orders."

**"It wasn't me jumping up and down and
yelling in class. It was the sugar talking."**

**"I have experience acting in loco parentis.
I'm dating a guy who still lives with
his parents."**

A.BACALL

"My name is Mrs. Clawson and I have a graduate degree in early childhood education . . . and a black belt in karate."

"I know that some of your students are very disruptive, but don't let your temper explode. Count down before blasting off."

"Shall we talk about your unacceptable behavior or shall we go directly to the penalty phase?"

"I have been controlling student behavior with a series of facial grimaces and contortions. Now I need a facial massage every week."

"Remember! I'm addressing your behavior, not your character. Although, you are a character."

**"My learning style involves acting up
from time to time."**

**"I wouldn't say your son is a bad child.
He's gifted at disruptive behavior."**

PLAYING THE SANTA CARD

"My teacher said if I continue to be disruptive in class, she will tell Santa that I'm naughty. Then he will bring me only educational toys."

"I am homeschooling you. That doesn't mean you can misbehave in class. If you keep calling out, I will have to call your mother and report my concerns to myself."

"I don't need to go to a gym. One of
my classroom management strategies
is to circulate frequently around the room.
I figure I walk three miles a day."

"You have been acting out every day this week. If you promise to sit quietly in class, I will help you apply for a Screen Actors Guild card."

"Sorry for being so cranky. I underslept again."

"Frequent and effective communication is the foundation of good classroom management. That is why I send a daily behavior report to all parents of my students. The postage is expensive but the silence is golden."

"Do you have any books on managing disruptive students? I want to know what the opposition is up to."

**"If you want to communicate with a disruptive
student, learn to hear what isn't being said."**

"If you have a student who refuses to stay seated, put that behavior to work delivering messages for you, collecting completed work, handing out and collecting books, and taking around the wastebasket."

Applying yoga principles to classroom management

A.BACALL

"Tranquility can be reached by allowing the mind to be quiet. True tranquility can be achieved by allowing the mouth to be quiet."

"That's my survival kit. It has a meditation tape, aspirin, and rose-colored glasses."

"Every day it's the same thing. My class starts out as Sesame Street and by three o'clock it ends up as Jerry Springer."

**"If you don't come to class, you
don't get to pass."**

"I circulate around the classroom all day to make sure the class runs smoothly. I need a pair of comfortable walking shoes."

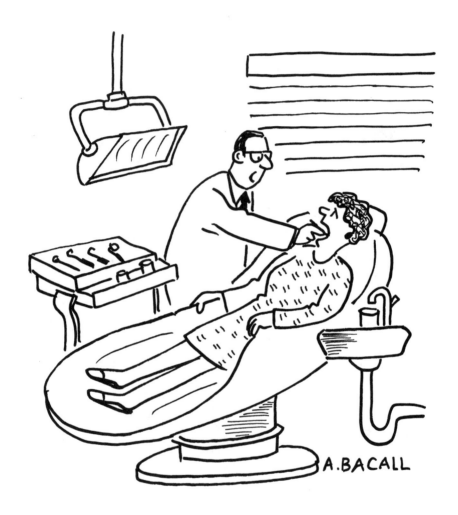

"I have a waiting room filled with people that have different needs and don't want to be here. You're a teacher. You wouldn't know how stressful that is."

"I keep calling the homes of my disruptive students, but when all is said and done, more is said than done."

"I am very proud to hear that my son is the class clown."

THE NIGHT BEFORE THE CLASS FIELD TRIP

A.BACALL

"Please let the bus show up on time. Please let all the students bring their lunch money. Please let there be enough parent volunteers. Please let the weather cooperate."

**"We do not permit bullying or name calling
in our school. We will reprimand any student
that calls your child a dummy."**

"Your son enjoys hands-on activities, but he has to learn to keep his hands to himself."

"I wouldn't say your son's behavior has improved. It's just different. He stopped passing notes to friends in class. Now he's text-messaging them."

"You managed to stretch the proverbial fifteen minutes in the limelight into a full hour. Now sit down and stop acting up!"

"Good-bye tension. Hello pension!"

CORWIN
PRESS

The Corwin Press logo—a raven striding across an open book—represents the union of courage and learning. Corwin Press is committed to improving education for all learners by publishing books and other professional development resources for those serving the field of PreK–12 education. By providing practical, hands-on materials, Corwin Press continues to carry out the promise of its motto: **"Helping Educators Do Their Work Better."**